LOOK CLOSER

SHORELINE

PHOTOGRAPHED BY
FRANK GREENAWAY

WRITTEN BY
BARBARA TAYLOR

DORLING KINDERSLEY
LONDON • NEW YORK • STUTTGART

[DK]

A DORLING KINDERSLEY BOOK

Editor Sue Copsey **Art editor** Val Wright
Senior editor Christiane Gunzi **Designer** Floyd Sayers
Design assistants Nicola Rawson, Lucy Bennett
Production Louise Barratt
Illustrations Nick Hall
Index Jane Parker
Managing editor Sophie Mitchell
Managing art editor Miranda Kennedy
U.S. editor B. Alison Weir

Consultants
Geoff Boxshall, Barry Clarke, Theresa Greenaway,
Gordon Howes, Tim Parmenter, Edward Wade, Kathie Way

With special thanks to Robin James, Mike Quorm, and
all the staff of Weymouth Sea Life Centre, and to
Mark Jones for supplying some of the animals in this book.

First American Edition, 1993
10 9 8 7 6 5 4 3 2 1
Published in the United States by
Dorling Kindersley, Inc., 232 Madison Avenue, New York, New York, 10016

Published in Great Britain by Dorling Kindersley Limited.
Distributed by Houghton Mifflin Company, Boston, Massachusetts.

Library of Congress Cataloging-in-Publication Data
Taylor, Barbara 1954-
Shoreline/Barbara Taylor ; photography by Frank Greenaway. –1st American ed.
p. cm. – (Look closer)
Includes index.
Summary: Discusses the animals and plants that live at the edge of the sea.
Includes queen scallops, hermit crabs, and various shoreline plants.
ISBN 1-56458-213-2
1. Seashore biology–Juvenile literature. 2. Seashore fauna–Juvenile literature.
3. Seashore plants–Juvenile literature.
[1. Seashore animals. 2. Seashore plants.] I. Greenaway, Frank, ill. II. Title. III. Series.
QH95.7.T39. 1993
574.909'46–dc20
92-53491-CIP-AC
Color reproduction by Colourscan, Singapore
Printed and bound in Italy by New Interlitho, Milan

CONTENTS

Look for us, and we will show you the size of every animal and plant that you read about in this book.

LIFE ON THE SHORE

WHERE THE LAND MEETS the sea and forms sandy or rocky shores, all kinds of wildlife make their homes. Many crabs, worms, fish, and plants have adapted to life in this salty environment, where there is little fresh water. Some shoreline plants and animals live so close to the sea that the tide washes over them twice a day. They have to be able to survive in both wet and dry conditions. Today, shorelines all over the world are threatened by pollution from oil spills, factory waste, and litter left by people. We need to keep our beaches clean and remember that we share them with the wildlife that lives there.

The queen scallop's
(Chlamys opercularis)
shell is 3 1/2 in. wide.
It lives in north-western Europe.

The hermit crab's
(Pagurus bernhardus)
body is 4 in. long.
It lives in Europe, North America, and Scandinavia.

The tub gurnard
(Trigla lucerna)
is 1 ft. long.
It lives in Europe.

The peacock worm's
(Sabella pavonina)
body is 10 in. long.
It lives in Europe.

The lesser weever fish
(Trachinus vipera)
is 4 3/4 in. long.
It lives in Europe and North America.

The king ragworm
(Nereis virens)
is 1 ft. long.
It lives in North America, Northeast Asia, and northern Europe.

The common lizard
(Lacerta vivipara)
is 6 in. long.
It lives in central and
northern Europe, and
northern Asia.

The oystercatcher
(Haematopus ostralegus)
is 17 in. long.
It lives in Europe, India,
Northwest Africa,
Scandinavia, and the
Middle East.

The thrift's
(Armeria maritima)
flower stem is 3 1/2 in.
high, and its flowers
are 1/2 in. wide.
It lives north of
the equator.

The natterjack toad
(Bufo calamita)
is 2 1/2 in. long.
It lives in Europe.

The sea pea's
(Lathyrus japonicus [maritimus])
flower stem is 4 in. high, and its
flowers are 1/2 in. wide.
It lives in North America, northern
Asia, and northern Europe.

WRIGGLING WORMS

THESE COLORFUL KING ragworms get their name from the ragged fringe of flat legs, called parapodia, along the sides of their bodies. Ragworms often live in burrows beneath the surface of the sand, and they wriggle around to keep a current of water flowing past. Water contains oxygen, which a ragworm needs in order to breathe. The water also carries scents and tastes from above the sand. When the ragworm senses prey, it shoots out of its burrow to grab it. In the breeding season, female king ragworms lay eggs on the seabed, and the males fertilize them. Then all the adults die. Their eggs develop into tiny larvae that swim around, feeding on plankton, while they grow and develop. After about two years, they will be fully grown adults, living in the sand.

GUESS WHAT?
These animals are called king ragworms because they can grow so large. An adult can be up to 3 ft. long, and wider than a ruler.

TINY TENTACLES
Each body segment has a pair of flat, paddlelike parapodia. The ragworm uses these for crawling, swimming, and breathing. They work like the gills of a fish to take in oxygen from the water. Each one has two small, feelerlike cirri, and two bundles of stiff bristles, for gripping surfaces.

These iridescent violet colors are made by light reflecting off both sides of the worm's thin skin.

The body is made up of more than 100 segments.

FOOD FINDERS

On the ragworm's head there are many sense organs. These help the worm to hunt for food, and pick up information about its environment. The four eyes, two palps, and two short antennae are sensitive to light, smell, and touch. There are also four tentacles that can feel things.

SHRINKING WORM

To escape from enemies, such as birds, the king ragworm contracts (tightens) the muscles that run from its head to its tail. This makes its body much shorter, so the ragworm can move backward suddenly, or disappear into its burrow quickly.

These two short antennae, and the two palps, help the worm find food. The mouth is on the underside of the head.

If king ragworms lose their tentacles, they can grow new ones.

PINCER POWER

The king ragworm is an omnivore, which means that it feeds on almost anything it can find, such as fish eggs, larvae, and plant and animal remains. This animal is a fierce hunter, seizing prey with its strong, pincerlike jaws. There are six to ten teeth on each jaw.

The bristles on the parapodia can spread out like a fan to help the worm grip the sand and mud.

The worm's body is flat, so it can crawl into cracks and under stones, and slide through the sand easily.

MOBILE HOME

THIS BRIGHTLY COLORED hermit crab rips its food apart with its sharp pincers. Hermit crabs are scavengers, feeding mainly on the remains of dead animals. They crawl around on the shoreline, pulling themselves along with the strong front legs that stick out of their shell. A hermit crab does not have a hard outer layer on its abdomen (the rear part of the body) as most crabs do. So it finds an empty shell, such as this whelk shell, to live in. As the hermit crab grows bigger, it changes its shell for a larger one. Hermit crabs come out of their shells to mate. Then the female carries her eggs around with her inside her shell until they hatch. The tiny larvae join the mass of plankton floating and feeding near the surface of the sea. Several weeks later they sink to the seabed, where they search for a small, empty shell to use as their first home.

GUESS WHAT?
If a hermit crab damages one of its legs, it sheds it and grows a new one in its place.

A FOOT IN THE DOOR
If a hermit crab is attacked by an enemy, such as a seabird, it quickly pulls itself deep inside its shell. Then the crab wedges the larger of its two front pincers across the opening of its shell. This seals off the entrance, just like an armor-plated door.

These legs end in sharp claws for gripping onto the seabed.

The crab's outer skin, called the exoskeleton, is hard at the front in order to protect the exposed parts of the body.

Each eye is on the end of a long stalk.

The hermit crab uses its two front pairs of legs for walking, and drags its home behind it wherever it goes.

These two short feelers, called antennules, are sensitive to touch.

HITCHING A RIDE

Barnacles, sea anemones, and sponges often live on top of a hermit crab's shell. These animals cannot move by themselves, but the crab carries them around to new feeding areas. In return, they disguise the crab's shell as it moves around on the seabed. The stinging tentacles of the anemones also help ward off the crab's enemies.

These long, flexible antennae (feelers) smell the water for food.

BED AND BREAKFAST

If you look closely, you can see that a ragworm has wriggled up from inside the hermit crab's shell to share its meal. This kind of ragworm often lives inside the shells of hermit crabs. There it does not have to search for food, and it is safe from birds and other enemies.

Feathery mouthparts pass small pieces of food toward the mouth.

Close up, you can see the ragworm inside this hermit crab's shell.

14

FISH FINGERS

TUB GURNARDS WALK slowly over the ocean floor on their fins. They use the fingerlike rays at the front of their pectoral fins to push themselves along. These fish usually live in small groups, called schools, in shallow water near the shore. There they search for food in the sand, mud, and pebbles. Tub gurnards eat many kinds of small fish, as well as shrimps, crabs, and sea-dwelling worms. In summer, each female gurnard lays thousands of tiny eggs that measure less than a millimeter across. At first, the young that hatch out of the eggs float in the water close to the surface. But there they are easy prey for larger fish. So when the surviving young are fully developed, they swim down into the ocean to begin their adult lives.

GUESS WHAT?
Gurnards get their name from the French word "grogner," which means "to grunt." This is because of the loud grunts that these fish make to communicate with each other.

COLOR CHANGE
This young tub gurnard's pectoral fins have bright blue edges and greenish-blue spots at the base. As the fish grows larger, these striking colors will change. A fully grown tub gurnard has brilliant red and blue pectoral fins with green edges.

The fish uses these large pectoral fins for balancing and turning.

The pointed snout is a good shape for scooping up food from the seabed.

The dorsal fin stands up to keep the fish steady in the water.

Mottled brown colors help the fish blend in with the sand and shingle of the sea floor.

The tail fin pushes the fish through the water.

There are no scales on the head. Instead, it is protected by small, bony plates and spines.

FEELING FINS

The three rays at the front of each pectoral fin work like feelers. The tub gurnard uses them for walking, and for poking around for food on the seabed. They are separate from the rest of the rays on the fin, which are joined together by a thin skin, called a membrane. Each of the front rays can move on its own, the same way your fingers do.

Like all fish, the gurnard breathes through gills. These are under the bony gill covers on each side of its head.

A sensitive organ, called the lateral line, runs down each side of the body. This detects movements in the water.

Fishes' eyes do not have eyelids. Instead, seawater keeps them moist and clean.

If danger threatens, the pectoral fins flick sand and gravel over the body to hide it from enemies.

16

A PLACE IN THE SUN

COMMON LIZARDS CAN slip easily through clumps of grass on the shore, hunting for insects and spiders to eat. Like all reptiles, lizards need to be warm in order to move around, and they often stretch out on the sand to bask in the sunshine. Winter is too cold for them, and food is short, so they find a sheltered place, such as a burrow, where they can hibernate (sleep). In spring, common lizards form pairs for mating. The female finds a damp place in the sand and lays 4 to 11 eggs, which are protected by a transparent (see-through) membrane. The young soon emerge and run around, feeding on spiders and insects, such as flies. The adults take little interest in their young, and many of them are eaten by snakes, birds, or mammals.

An eyelid wipes over each eye to keep it clean.

The colors and patterns on the lizard's scales help hide it from both predators and prey.

Like most reptiles, lizards shed their skin in order to grow.

The lizard's nostrils are on the tip of its snout.

Strong jaws grab and hold prey tight.

SIXTH SENSE
The common lizard belongs to a group of animals called reptiles. Like most animals, reptiles can see, hear, feel, taste, and smell. They also have a forked tongue, which picks up chemical information from the air. A special organ in the roof of the mouth uses the information to build up an image of the animal's surroundings. This organ is called the Jacobson's organ.

GUESS WHAT?
Unlike most reptiles, this lizard's young are fully formed by the time it lays the egg sacs. Instead of a hard shell, they only have to break out of a thin, baglike membrane.

QUICK AS A FLASH
The common lizard chases prey among the sand dunes until it gets very close. Then at the last moment, it darts forward to seize the animal in its strong jaws.

Lizards have good eyesight, and they can see in color.

These long, strong toes grip surfaces well. Lizards are good at climbing.

Close up, you can see a small ear opening on the side of the head.

The long, thin body slides easily through grass and under stones.

A LUCKY BREAK
If an enemy grabs the lizard's tail, it has a very useful trick for escaping. It simply breaks off part of its tail and runs away. There are special weak points in the tail, so it does not hurt if it breaks off. A new tail gradually grows, although it does not have weak points like the old one.

Most of the bones in the tail can easily break apart, allowing the lizard to escape from a predator's grip.

The tail is often longer than the body. The lizard uses it for swimming, and to help balance its body when it is running or climbing.

A FOREST OF FANS

AT LOW TIDE, PEACOCK worms look like tiny, muddy pipes sticking out of the beach. But when the tide comes in and covers them with water, beautiful feathery fans spread out from the ends of each tube. These fans are the gills of peacock worms. A peacock worm's soft body is hidden inside its long, protective tube, which it builds from mud and sand. Each tube sticks up about 4 in. above the shore, but there may be another 16 in. hidden in the sand below. The body is divided into hundreds of segments, like the body of an earthworm. In spring and summer, peacock worms release many tiny eggs into the water. These eggs hatch into larvae that drift in the ocean with the plankton. After about two weeks, they settle down on the shore, where they each build a tube to live in.

GUESS WHAT?
This worm's fan of gills looks sort of like a peacock's fan of tail feathers. That is why these worms are known as peacock worms.

The gills are for breathing, as well as for catching food.

The worm makes its tube from mud and sand, cemented together with slimy mucus.

The worm's mouth is hidden in the center of its gills.

The gills sense movements in the water and changes in light and dark.

FOOD FAN
The feathery gills catch tiny water creatures and scraps of food floating past in the water. Each gill pushes food toward the worm's mouth, which is at the center of the fan. The gills also trap tiny particles of sand and mud.

In times of danger, and when the tide is out, the worm pulls its head and gills back inside the tube.

MUD AND SLIME
A peacock worm builds its smooth, rounded tube out of tiny pieces of mud and fine sand. It sticks them together with a slimy substance called mucus, which it makes in its body. The inside of the tube is lined with mucus, so that the worm can slide up and down easily.

Close up, you can see fringes of tiny hairs, called cilia. These help trap food and move it toward the mouth.

The fan is divided into two semi-circles. Each of these has between 8 and 45 gills.

LYING LOW
Peacock worms are usually covered by water. When they are exposed to the air at low tide, the worms go right down to the bottom of their tubes. There they stay cool, damp, and safe from enemies.

The gills can be all sorts of colors, such as brown, red, or purple. They usually have darker bands of color running through them.

The lower end of the tube is usually attached to pebbles beneath the sand. This keeps it firmly in place when waves wash over it.

BURIED ALIVE

IN CLEAR, SHALLOW water close to the shore, the lesser weever fish lies waiting for a meal to pass by. It often lies almost completely buried, with just its eyes, mouth, and poisonous dorsal fin poking out of the sand or shingle. This means that the fish can see, catch food, and defend itself while most of its body is hidden. In summer, the weever fish moves up and down the shore as the tide goes in and out. It spends winter in deeper waters, farther out to sea, where it can avoid the rough waves that bad weather brings to the coast. The female weever spawns (lays her eggs) in summer. Each tiny egg has a number of yellow oil droplets inside, which keep it from sinking. After about ten days, the eggs hatch into young that float in the sea with the plankton. When the young are fully developed, they leave the surface of the ocean and swim down to the sea floor.

STINGING FINS
If the weever is alarmed or attacked by an enemy, such as a flatfish, it raises the fanlike fin on its back. This fin, called the dorsal fin, is supported by several sharp spines. At the base of these spines there are sacs of poison. If the weever needs to defend itself, it injects poison into the enemy through its sharp spines.

Mottled yellow and brown colors on the body blend in with the sea floor. This helps the fish hide from enemies and prey.

These rounded side fins, called pectoral fins, are for pushing and steering the fish through the water. They also dig holes in the seabed.

SANDY SECRETS
The weever fish digs itself a shallow dip in the seabed with the fins at the front of its body. It also blows sand out of the way with the water that passes out of its gills. Then it lies in wait, ready to ambush prey, such as shrimp, shore crabs, and worms.

This long fin along the back is supported by about 25 bony rays. There is a similar fin underneath the body.

GUESS WHAT?

Sometimes people step on weever fish buried beneath the sand of the seashore. If the poisonous spines on the dorsal fin pierce the skin, they cause a painful sting.

WATER WORKS

Like all fish, the weever breathes through gills. These work like our lungs to take in oxygen from the water. The weever opens and shuts its mouth all the time, drawing in water. Then it forces the water out again past the gills and the bony gill covers on each side of its head.

Overlapping scales cover and protect the body. They are thin, light, and flexible, so the fish can move easily.

Spines on this small black fin inject poison into attackers. The poison runs along grooves in the spines.

The large mouth sweeps upward out of the sand and gravel to catch food. It also gulps down water for breathing.

A bony cover, called the operculum, protects the delicate gills underneath.

PIED PIPER

THE OYSTERCATCHER'S loud, piping call and black-and-white pied feathers make it easy to find on the shoreline. As the name suggests, oystercatchers feed mainly on oysters and other mollusks, but they also eat small crabs, shrimps, and worms. In autumn and winter, these birds live in large groups, called flocks. In spring and summer, they form pairs and find a small area on the shore, called a territory, where they lay their eggs. A female lays two to four eggs in a shallow hole, called a scrape. The male and female take turns sitting on the eggs, which hatch after about four weeks. The chicks can run around soon after hatching, but they rely on their parents to feed them for several weeks, or even months.

GUESS WHAT?
Sometimes the two halves of a sea creature's shell may shut tightly, trapping an oystercatcher's bill before it has managed to break the shell apart. The bird can get free only by cracking the shell against a stone until it opens.

SPOT THE EGG
The colors and patterns on the oystercatcher's eggs make them look like pebbles, so they are difficult for enemies to spot. Oystercatchers sometimes try to fool an enemy by getting off their eggs and pretending to sit on them somewhere else.

The nostrils are high up, so they do not become clogged with sand when the bird is digging for food.

The tip of the bill is narrow and strong, for prying the two halves of a shell apart.

This joint looks like a knee, but it is really an ankle.

The feet spread wide so that the oystercatcher does not sink as it walks on wet sand.

The speckled eggs blend in well with the pebbles, which makes it difficult for enemies to find them.

A SMASHING BILL

An oystercatcher's long, blunt bill is specially adapted for breaking open shells. It levers them off rocks, and pries or smashes them open. When the bird finds an open shell, it pushes its bill between the two halves and cuts the muscle that holds them together. If the shell is closed, the bird hammers away at one side with its bill until it breaks through to the soft flesh inside.

A thick covering of waterproof feathers on the body keeps it warm and dry.

NOISY NEIGHBORS

During the breeding season, oystercatchers become very noisy, as each pair claims its own territory on the shore. All the birds rush around with their bills pointing down toward the ground, making shrill piping calls. These loud messages warn other birds to keep away.

The tail feathers help the oystercatcher to steer in the air. They also balance the weight of the bird's body when it perches or sits on the ground.

SHARING THE SHORE

An oystercatcher is just one of the many kinds of birds that poke about on the shoreline looking for food. Each kind of bird has a different size or shape of bill so that it can find food at different depths in the mud or sand. In this way, the birds share the rich food supply, and many different kinds of birds can live close together.

TOAD IN THE HOLE

DURING THE DAY, the natterjack toad stays inside its sandy burrow. When night falls, the toad creeps out of its hiding place to hunt for insects in the cool, damp air. Natterjack toads hibernate (sleep) during the cold winter months, burying themselves deep in the sand. In spring they migrate to fresh water nearby, where they breed. The males croak loudly to attract females. After mating, the females lay strings of eggs about six feet long in the water. Each string may contain up to 4,000 eggs. Five to ten days later, tadpoles hatch out of the eggs and swim around, feeding mainly on algae (simple plants). After six to eight weeks they have changed into tiny toads measuring less than a half inch long. Now they are ready to leave the water and begin life on the shore. It will take four or five years for these young toads to become fully grown.

GUESS WHAT?
Toads can survive away from water for much longer than frogs. But their skin can easily dry out, so they stay cool below the surface of the sand during the day.

HUNGRY HUNTER
Natterjack toads feed mainly on insects, especially ants and beetles. They have huge appetites, and may eat hundreds of insects in one night. The toad flicks out its tongue at an insect, catching it on the sticky tip. As the toad swallows the prey, it blinks. This forces its eyes down into the head, and helps push food down the throat.

PEELING OFF
The natterjack toad breathes with its lungs, and also through its skin. So it is important that the skin stays in good condition. Like frogs and other amphibians, the toad molts (sheds its skin) every five or six days. It peels off the old skin with its mouth and front feet, to reveal a shiny new skin underneath. Natterjack toads usually eat their old skin.

LITTLE LEGS
Natterjack toads have much shorter back legs than most other toads and frogs. They cannot swim or jump as well as their relatives, but they are surprisingly nimble, and are good at walking and running.

Natterjack toads are sometimes called golden backs, because of this narrow yellow line along the back.

Bulging eyes give the toad a wide field of vision.

Nostrils take air into the lungs.

Strong front legs are used for burrowing into sand.

Short back legs can walk and run quickly.

The toes are webbed and widely splayed. This is a good shape for shoveling sand.

DO NOT DISTURB

If the natterjack toad spots a predator, such as a bird, it can puff up its body and straighten its back legs to make itself look taller, fatter, and fiercer. This is often enough to stop the animal from attacking the toad. But if a predator does grab it, a foul-tasting poison oozes out from the parotoid glands behind its eyes. Most animals quickly drop the toad and look for a tastier meal instead.

A round, flat eardrum on each side of the head picks up sounds.

These large lumps are parotoid glands full of poison, which oozes out if an enemy attacks the toad.

Patterns and bumps on the skin help the toad blend in with its sandy surroundings.

SEASIDE FLAPPERS

QUEEN SCALLOPS LIE on the muddy seabed close to the shore feeding on tiny sea plants. They live in large groups, called colonies. Scallops are much better swimmers than other shelled sea creatures, such as mussels. They flap along through the water in a series of jerks. The two halves of a scallop's shell are called valves. They are strong and hard, and protect the soft body inside. In summer, scallops release clouds of eggs into the water. A tiny larva hatches out of each egg and swims around for about three weeks. Then it anchors itself to a surface, such as a piece of seaweed, with strong threads that it produces inside its body. About a year later, when the shell is fully developed, the scallop swims off to join a colony of adults.

WATER JETS

Scallops swim by opening and shutting the two halves of their shell, much like clapping. This forces water out behind them in a strong jet, pushing them forward through the water. When danger threatens, queen scallops can shoot backward rapidly to escape.

The streamlined shape of the shell cuts through the water easily. This means that the scallop can quickly swim away from a lurking starfish.

These ridges running across the shell can tell you how old the scallop is.

About 20 broad ribs fan out from the bottom of the shell to make it extra strong.

Starfish like to eat scallops. They are strong enough to pull the two valves apart to reach the soft body inside.

Scallops swim by "clapping" the two parts of their shell.

SEAFOOD SUPPER

Queen scallops lie on the sea floor with their shells open, waiting for food to float past. They trap tiny plants, called algae, in the waving hairs on their gills. These hairs work like a sieve to filter food from the water.

The two valves are joined together with a strong elastic substance, called ligament.

Barnacles often grow on top of scallop shells. They help disguise the scallops as they lie on the seabed.

GUESS WHAT?
Sea creatures that live in shells are often called shellfish. But they are not related to fish. Scallops are mollusks, and are related to the slugs and snails that live in gardens.

A WRINKLY QUEEN
As the soft body of the queen scallop grows, its shell gets bigger, too. The speed at which the shell grows depends on certain things, such as changes in temperature. This speeding up and slowing down causes ridges on the shell, which are sort of like the rings in a tree trunk. The more ridges you count, the older the scallop. Queen scallops can live for up to eight years.

These tiny, sensitive tentacles can detect enemies, such as starfish.

Shelled sea creatures that have two halves to their shell, such as scallops and mussels, are called bivalves.

These rows of small, simple eyes can detect moving objects and changes in light and dark.

The mottled colors of the shell blend in with the sand and gravel. This makes it difficult for enemies, such as seabirds, to spot the scallop.

A SPLASH OF COLOR

IN SUMMER, SEA PEAS and thrift bring patches of bright color to the shoreline. These plants grow among the rocks and pebbles on the shore, and are able to survive the salty spray blowing in from the sea. Many shoreline plants, such as thrift and sea peas, have long roots to reach the rainwater that trickles between the pebbles and collects underground. These plants grow low on the ground, out of the wind. But thrift flowers have long stems, so when the wind blows, it shakes out the seeds. They fall to the ground and grow into new plants somewhere else along the shore.

Paper-thin sepals and delicate, leaf-like bracts protect each flower.

LEAFY CUSHIONS
The leaves of thrift grow in a low, grasslike cushion. Close to the ground, the plant can survive the constant buffeting of sea winds. The cushion also traps moisture, so any water vapor that escapes from the leaves is less likely to be blown away by the wind.

GUESS WHAT?
These plants look small because we can only see the part that is above ground. But thrift roots can grow to more than one yard long, and the creeping stems of a sea pea plant can be up to 2 1/2 ft. long.

FUNNY FLOWER
A sea pea flower is an unusual shape. It has a large petal at the top and a smaller one on either side. There are two more petals at the bottom that protect the pollen sacs and the female parts of the flower.

The thrift's narrow leaves grow close to the ground, where they are protected from the wind.

Sea pea flowers look similar to sweet pea flowers.

Each flower head is made up of several flowers at the top of a long, hairy stalk.

Thrift plants are also called sea pinks.

The five pollen sacs are at the center of each flower.

INDEX

GLOSSARY

Abdomen *the rear part of the body*
Algae *simple plants, such as seaweeds*
Antennae *a pair of feelers*
Barnacle *a small, shelled, sea-dwelling animal that attaches itself to rocks, plants, and other objects*
Bivalve *a mollusk, such as a scallop, which has a two-part, hinged shell*
Cilia *short, hairlike threads*
Exoskeleton *a tough covering on the body, made of a substance called chitin*
Gills *organs that animals, such as fish, use to take in oxygen from the water*
Gland *an organ that produces a chemical substance*
Hibernate *to rest or sleep during the cold months of the year*
Iridescent *shimmering with color, caused by light reflecting off two surfaces*
Larva *the young, grublike stage of an animal, such as an insect*

Lateral line *the line of sensitive cells along each side of a fish's body*
Migrate *to travel long distances to find food and a suitable place to breed*
Mollusk *a soft-bodied animal, such as a slug or snail, that often has a shell*
Mucus *a slimy, often poisonous substance that certain animals produce*
Omnivore *an animal that eats both plants and other animals*
Operculum *a protective cover, such as a fish's gill cover*
Parapodia *pairs of simple walking legs*
Pied *having two or more colors, usually black and white (animals)*
Plankton *tiny, floating sea creatures and plants*
Sepal *one of the outer parts of a flower that protects the bud*
Tentacles *flexible feelers for touching, feeding, or smelling*